# Oscar de Mejo's ABC

A Laura Geringer Book

*An Imprint of* HarperCollins*Publishers*

Notes from the letters A, B, F, H, I, N, O, T, S, U, V, Y, and Z were
taken from captions that originally appeared in *My America: Paintings and
Comments by Oscar de Mejo*, introductory text by Selden Rodman,
published by Harry N. Abrams, Inc., New York, 1983.
All rights reserved.

The painting for letter "Z" was a *Town & Country* magazine cover.

Oscar de Mejo's ABC
Copyright © 1992 by Oscar de Mejo
Printed in the U.S.A. All rights reserved.
Typography by Al Cetta
1   2   3   4   5   6   7   8   9   10
First Edition

Library of Congress Cataloging-in-Publication Data
De Mejo, Oscar.
  Oscar de Mejo's ABC / by Oscar de Mejo.
      p.    cm.
  "A Laura Geringer book."
  Summary: Paintings illustrate scenes from Americana for each
letter of the alphabet.
  ISBN 0-06-020516-4. — ISBN 0-06-020517-2 (lib. bdg.)
  1. United States—History—Juvenile literature.  2. English
language—Alphabet—Juvenile literature.  [1. United States—
History.  2. Alphabet.]  I. Title  II. Title: ABC.
E178.3.D4  1992                          91-28768
973—dc20                               CIP
                                           AC

*To Chiara and Pierpaolo with love*

# A  *America*

# B   *Boston Tea Party*

C *Cowboy*

D *Dance*

# E  *Eagle*

# F   *Flag*

# G   *George Washington*

# H  *Horse*

I    *Ice skaters*

J  *Jazz*

# K   *Kite*

L Lewis & Clark

# M  *Mother*

# N *Nap*

O   *Ocean*

P     *Patrick Henry*

Q    *Queen of Hearts*

# R  *Revolution*

## S   *Statue of Liberty*

T  *Train*

# U *Umpire*

# V  *Valley Forge*

W   *Wild West*

X   *Xmas*

# Y   *Yankees*

Z   *Zoo*

# A Message from Oscar de Mejo

## Here are the stories behind my paintings.

**A**—America. From the painting *Mother America*. 1973. Masonite, 18" x 14". Private collection, New York City.

Mother America is not to be taken lightly. Her sword vouches for that. But the justice she dispenses is equal for all. She has a very precise scale with which to measure it.

**B**—Boston Tea Party. From the painting *Boston Tea Party [1773]*. 1979. Canvas, 48" x 68". Collection Aberbach Fine Art, New York City.

Admiring bystanders watch as proper Bostonians, dressed as Indians, dump His Majesty's newly arrived tea into the harbor.

**C**—Cowboy. From the painting *Encounter With a Buffalo*. 1986. Canvas, 22" x 28". Collection Nahan Galleries, New Orleans.

The ferocious buffalo is getting ready to attack man and horse when the cowboy asks: "Hey, haven't we met before?" Stunned by the question, the buffalo turns around and leaves in a hurry.

**D**—Dance. From the painting *Masked Ball*. 1988. Canvas, 36" x 50". Collection Nahan Galleries, New Orleans.

Are all these people wearing a costume? Not all: America isn't. She was passing by as the party was in progress and decided to look in. The very patriotic host, Jefferson Maddox, shown dancing with her, could not be happier.

**E**—Eagle. From the painting *Victory Celebration*. 1984. Canvas, 36" x 50". Collection Aberbach Fine Art, New York City.

After the battle of Yorktown (1783), which concluded victoriously the American Revolution, the bald eagle is seen more and more often as the national emblem of the United States. My painting represents one of the many banquets given after the battle of Yorktown, and the centerpiece at the table is, naturally, a golden eagle.

**F**—Flag. From the painting *The General and the Seamstress [1776?]*. 1982. Canvas, 36" x 50". Collection Aberbach Fine Art, New York City.

This painting deals with the legend of Betsy Ross. General Washington has to choose the flag for his new army. "This is the one I want," he says, but then Betsy shows him one more flag, with one star surrounded by twelve stars in a circle. In the background on the wall is the coat of arms of the Washington family, placed there by the clever seamstress only minutes before the arrival of the general.

**G**—George Washington. From the painting *Meeting With George*. 1985. Canvas, 24" x 36". Collection Nahan Galleries, New Orleans.

These two great admirers of George Washington often stop in front of his portrait on the vase and talk to the Father of our Country. What they talk about is not known. But it is said that the great George sometimes answers from the vase with a brief "yes" or "no."

**H**—Horse. From the painting *The British Are Coming [1775]*. 1982. Canvas, 36" x 50". Collection Aberbach Fine Art, New York City.

Paul Revere is warning the countryside of approaching British soldiers. It is the start of the Revolutionary War.

**I**—Ice skaters. From the painting *The Happy Skaters*. 1979. Canvas, 36" x 50". Private collection, New York City.

This hotel facing the little lake of Bulwer-Lytton in Vermont is the winter headquarters of THE HARDER WE FALL, a club for skating enthusiasts. The founders of this club have a slogan which explains their philosophy—"The harder we fall, the better we feel"—and in order to demonstrate the soundness of their motto, the members skate with a vengeance, never giving thought to the possibility of falling flat on their faces. Not taking part in the fun is the mysterious lady who appears to be at least eight to ten feet tall (center, above train engine). Is she real?

**J**—Jazz. From the painting *Euterpe and Jazz Performers*. 1984. Canvas, 26" x 36". Collection Dorothy de Mejo, New York City.

In the twenties America presented to the world one of the most glorious musical gifts of the century—jazz. To me, jazz is a music phenomenon that can be compared to the Baroque music explosion of the 18th century. When I hear the trio and quartet of Benny Goodman I can't help thinking of the chamber music of Mozart, Vivaldi, Marcello, and Telemann played by *I Musici*. In my painting, Euterpe, the Muse of lyric poetry and music, materializes to crown with the laurel of fame two great jazz performers.

**K**—Kite. From the painting *Franklin and Kite*. 1976. Masonite, 15" x 18". Private collection, New York City.

Statesman, printer, scientist, and writer Benjamin Franklin experimented with electricity as early as the middle of the 18th century. From the dangerous experiment of flying a kite in a thunderstorm came his invention of the lightning rod.

**L**—Lewis & Clark. From the painting *Lewis & Clark [1804]*. 1974. Masonite, 20" x 26". Collection Bob Guccione and Kathy Keeton, New York City.

Thomas Jefferson's dream—the exploration of the west—materializes when Meriwether Lewis and William Clark leave St. Louis and follow the Missouri River. Despite a memorable encounter with a grizzly bear and minor mishaps, the expedition is a great success.

**M**—Mother. From the painting *Virginia Dare*. 1986. Canvas, 36" x 50". Collection John W. Kluge, Charlottesville, Virginia.

In my picture I show the birth of Virginia Dare (1587), first baby born in America of English parents. America, the future Republic, watches with interest from the window.

**N**—Nap. From the painting *Girl in Purple*. 1980. Canvas, 46" x 66". Private collection, New York City.

This girl whose name is Victoria has fallen asleep during her lunch hour while taking a rest in Central Park. She has been working as a seamstress in one of the largest department stores of New York, and although she is living in the Gay Nineties she is far from happy. She wants to be married to a rich man—a Rockefeller or a Vanderbilt—regretfully, those gentlemen never visit her store.

**O**—Ocean. From the painting *The Bon Homme Richard Attacks the H.M.S. Serapis [1779]*. 1979. Masonite, 24" x 30". Collection Aberbach Fine Art, New York City.

As the naval battle rages in the Atlantic Ocean near the coast of France, John Paul Jones, aboard *Bon Homme Richard*, is asked to surrender. He replies: "I have not yet begun to fight!" The battle lasts almost four hours, but in the end the Americans win and the British surrender.

**P**—Patrick Henry. From the painting *Liberty or Death*. 1986. Canvas, 38" x 48". Collection John W. Kluge, Charlottesville, Virginia.

In my picture I show Patrick Henry delivering his famous speech in Richmond, Virginia, at St. John's church on March 23, 1775. His words "Give me Liberty or give me Death" thrilled the American patriots and precipitated the rebellion in this state. The figure in green is a Minute Man. He hasn't got his uniform yet, so he wears his hunting clothes. It looks as if he came out of the flag he's holding to be present here. Incidentally, the slogan "Liberty or Death" was used on the flag of the Hanover Association during the Revolutionary War.

**Q**—Queen of Hearts. From the painting *The Game of Poker*. 1986. Canvas, 24" x 36". Collection Nahan Galleries, New Orleans.

At the New York flat of the King of Hearts, a high-stake poker game is in progress. The players—the King, the Queen, the Jack of Diamonds, and the Jolly Joker. At this moment, to the great disappointment of the King who has a straight flush in his hands, the Joker leaves the table to go to the bathroom.

**R**—Revolution. From the painting *Crossing the Delaware*. 1973. Masonite, 26" x 36". Collection Yorktown Victory Center, VA.

At the beginning of the Revolutionary War when Americans badly needed some good news about their fight with Britain, George Washington was able to supply some. Crossing the Delaware River secretly at night with some of his troops, Washington surprised in Trenton the mercenary army of Hessians who were fighting for the British. The battle which ensued was a complete success and gave the Americans a remarkable victory. In my picture I show Washington embarking with his army on barges that will take them on the hazardous trip. A divine hand from the sky gives a blessing to the daring American commander.

**S**—Statue of Liberty. From the painting *Over There*. 1975. Masonite, 20" x 26". Collection Bob Guccione and Kathy Keeton, New York City.

Both our Lord and the Lady with a torch witness the departure of American soldiers for Europe in 1917. A hand in the sky indicates where they are going—over there! They are going to write one more glorious page in the book of American history. As we know, this intervention of America precipitated events—the victory of the Allies ended World War I in just a year's time.

**T**—Train. From the painting *Iron Horse*. 1974. Masonite, 20" x 26". Collection Bob Guccione and Kathy Keeton, New York City.

In the picture I show an American businessman explaining to an Indian chief the advantages of a railroad train service. From the sky, Mercury, the ancient god of commerce, looks on benignly. "You won't need buffaloes and green pastures any longer," says the businessman. "Hmmm," comments the chief.

**U**—Umpire. From the painting *Tagged*. 1980. Masonite, 16" x 20". Private collection, New York City.

My picture shows a baseball game of the turn of the century, and the title explains the action. No different from today's action except for the players' outfits.

**V**—Valley Forge. From the painting *Valley Forge [1776]*. 1981. Canvas, 26" x 36". Collection Aberbach Fine Art, New York City.

Shown here is the hardship of the newly born American army at the beginning of the Revolution. The tall French officer on the left is America's friend and ally, the Marquis de Lafayette. The two bundled-up figures next to him are Martha and George Washington on an impromptu visit from their Philadelphia home. They watch Baron von Steuben drill the troops.

**W**—Wild West. From the painting *The Indian Attack*. 1975. Masonite, 20" x 26". Collection Bob Guccione and Kathy Keeton, New York City.

The trip west was not always easy. Here, bullets and arrows are flying in both directions. Chronicles of the times tell of unscrupulous merchants selling the best Winchesters on the market to both sides.

**X**—Xmas. From the painting *Christmas in Africa*. 1988. Canvas, 18" x 22". Collection Nahan Galleries, New Orleans.

A group of European visitors are celebrating in Africa their Christmas European-fashion. A friendly lion was asked to help decorate the Christmas tree and he promptly obliged.

**Y**—Yankees. From the painting *Incident at Bull Run [1861]*. 1974. Masonite, 20" x 26". Collection Bob Guccione and Kathy Keeton, New York City.

In the first battle of the Civil War, a group of Union soldiers is ambushed by Confederate sharpshooters.

**Z**—Zoo. From the painting *Animals in Captivity*. 1975. Masonite, 26" x 36". Private collection, New York City.

The father takes his little girl to the zoo. "Too bad mother could not come," says the girl. "Yes," says the father. But she is with them in spirit.